florists' review

Design
School

Front cover and back cover floral arrangement displayed on Page 32.

Introduction

Florists' Review: Design School is a guide to the practice of floral artistry. For the novice or professional florist, this book explores concepts of embracing personal creativity, practicing the design process, reviewing the principles and elements of design, and developing skilled techniques. Furthermore, this book outlines floral arrangement styles and their historical associations for floral designers to develop a continued practice and study of the art form.

Be inspired by fellow designers! Throughout the book, you will see images from various floral artists who highlight their mastered skills in creation of floral art. It is important to learn from other floral designers to assist in your personal practice of artistry. Ergo, under many of the images, descriptions from the florists are provided to review their process of creation.

Note that all botanical materials listed within the text are written with their scientific Latin names to ensure clarity and proper notation. Furthermore, the common term for describing the arranging of flowers – *floral design* – is also referred to here as *floral art, floral arrangement,* and *botanical artistry*, interchangeably.

(opposite page)
DESIGNER: Françoise Weeks
RECIPE: *Papaver nudicaule, Ranunculus asiaticus, Tulipa* spp.*, Ceropegia linearis, Pieris japonica, Rubus* spp.*, Echeveria* spp.,
Berzelia lanuginosa, Adiantum capillus-veneris, Petroselinum crispum, Maranta leuconeura, Begonia spp.
"Typically I use few flowers when designing woodlands; textures - interesting foliage, succulents, berries and
seed pods - always reign; however, this tall rough piece of wood needed to be softened and brightened up a bit.
A few strings of *Ceropegia* along with dancing *Papaver*, a few bicolor *Ranunculus* and *Tulipa* did the trick."
PHOTOGRAPHER: Joni Shimabukuro

contents

DESIGNER: The Flori.Culture
RECIPE: *Citrus × aurantiifolia, Kalanchoe blossfeldiana, Malus domestica, Pieris japonica, Syringa vulgaris*
"This farm fresh aesthetic is the perfect floral décor for a low-key spring or summer gathering."
PHOTOGRAPHER: Macey Sierka

CREATIVITY

Develop Innovative Works

/creativity/

the product of original thought, finding alternatives, or exploring new possibilities through imagination and innovation.

Creativity is **experience.**

Creativity is discovery.

Creativity is **inspiration.**

Creativity is innovation.

For a florist, practicing creativity is an essential component to the development of personal botanical artistic expression. If we do not exercise our creative minds, we are simply placing flowers in a vase or replicating other designers' styles. What is the fun in that? Thus, though this book reviews the essential components in the process of mastering the art of floral design, take these learned concepts and interpret them into your own artistic perspective.

WAYS TO DEVELOP A CREATIVE FLORAL PRACTICE

- **Dedicate the time** to design for personal satisfaction. Cultivate and perfect your skill set.

- Incorporate a **personal space** for your own creative outlet.

- **Be engaged and mindful** throughout the design process.

- **Play with and manipulate** botanical materials. After an event or photo shoot, repurpose your design, and see what you can come up with.

- **Borrow ideas** from other designs, **but discover new possibilities** within this imitation process.

- **Embrace your constraints**, and use them to your advantage.

- Design styles that are **joyful and amusing** to you.

- Design styles that are **complicated and foreign** to you.

- **Evaluate the design** upon completion – explore your innovation and find meaning.

- **Practice** the "Design Process" *(see Page 9).*

DESIGN KNOWLEDGE
Hone Creativity Through Process

DESIGNER/PHOTOGRAPHER: Floral Art LA
RECIPE: *Aralia spinosa, Hydrangea macrophylla, Phalaenopsis amabilis, Xanthorrhoea johnsonii*
"This hedge arrangement combines the architectural lines of steel grass with a base of fluffy *Hydrangea*, delicately accented with *Phalaenopsis.*"

The verb *"design"* means *to execute a plan in the creation of a project.* In the case of floral design, the designer must plan the details of an arrangement before placing stems in a vase, just as any other artist must do with any other medium. First giving thought to botanical materials, color story, vessel and setting is necessary to determine the meaning of the arrangement. The "Design Process Blueprint" on the opposite page is a helpful tool to assist artisans through the stages of creative arranging.

DESIGN PROCESS
Design Process Blueprint for Floral Design

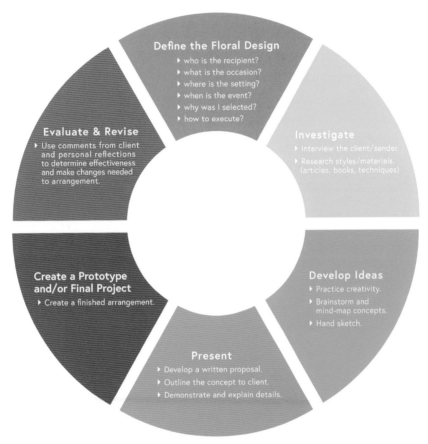

This figure was adapted and based on "The Design Process Outline" *(Vande Zande et al., 2014).*
Used with permission of the National Art Education Association ©2014. Adapted and retrieved from "The Design Process in the Art Classroom: Building Problem Solving Skills for Life and Careers" *(Vande Zande et al., 2014).*

How do I use this blueprint?

Begin working through the blueprint under "Define the Floral Design" on the top of the diagram. Define the arrangement using the questions who, what, where, when, why, and how. Then work your way through each stage within the circle – in your own order (Investigate, Develop Ideas, Present, Create Prototype and/or Final Product, Evaluate, and Revise). This formula will assist you in developing a creative, well-developed floral arrangement for your clients – no matter the occasion.

This framework presents the stages in a circular formation, allowing the artist to work sequentially or nonsequentially through each stage, depending on preference. Because the activity of design is neither static nor formulaic, this framework is open ended, allowing one to find intent, use imagination and harness knowledge to generate a completed artwork.

ABOUT THE ELEMENTS AND PRINCIPLES

What are they?

DESIGNER: The Flori.Culture
RECIPE: *Rosa* spp.
"We call these little copper bud vases 'the penny.' They are so simple yet elegant and can be placed in a series along a tablescape or as an accent on a coffee table."
PHOTOGRAPHER: Macey Sierka

The elements and principles of design are the components that make up a piece of artwork. Essentially, they are the building blocks and tools to all art forms. Every piece of art has them. A painting, a sculpture, or a floral arrangement each contain all of the elements and principles. Knowing and understanding how artists of a particular medium apply the principles and elements of design will assist you in developing artistic appreciation and knowledge of the medium.

/elements/

the tangible ingredients found within a floral arrangement

Color, Form, Fragrance, Line, Size, Space, Texture

/principles/

standards to follow in the organization of the elements

Balance, Dominance, Harmony, Proportion, Scale, Rhythm, Unity

ELEMENTS OF DESIGN

Color, Form, Fragrance, Line, Size, Space, Texture

The elements are building blocks to creating art. Every floral arrangement contains all of the elements, yet labeling each element within a specific design is unique to that piece. Knowing how to work with each of these elements allows us to proceed into the process of creating a well-developed floral design.

DESIGNER: The Flori.Culture
RECIPE: *Acacia* spp., *Aster pringlei, Craspedia variabilis, Echeveria* spp., *Eryngium amethystinum, Leucospermum* spp., *Ornithogalum dubium, Ranunculus asiaticus, Rosa* spp., *Serruria florida*
"This centerpiece is popular for events we design for in Arizona because the hues reflect our Southwest sunsets.
The color scheme comprises sunset hues, including warm reds, pinks, oranges, and yellows contrasted with cool blues and violets.
This arrangement is 'polychromatic' because almost all colors on the color wheel are incorporated."
PHOTOGRAPHER: Macey Sierka

DESIGNER: The Flori.Culture
RECIPE: *Ranunculus asiaticus, Rosa* spp., *Tulipa* spp.
"This design screams wedding! At The Flori.Culture, we love using soft pastel tints for wedding arrangements, and this blush, soft peach and cream design is the perfect color story for a spring wedding."
PHOTOGRAPHER: Charity Maurer

COLOR
[element]

Color matters. Of all the elements, color undoubtedly draws the most immediate attention and causes the strongest response from the viewer.

However, color preferences are subjective. Everyone has color choice preferences based on personality or cultural background. Therefore, floral designers must comprehend this sensitivity and design with versatility.

PRIMARY ▸ RED | YELLOW | BLUE

Basic colors for the creation of all other colors. In combination with each other or with white or black, all other hues are formed.

SECONDARY ▸ ORANGE | GREEN | VIOLET

Created by combining equal parts of two primary colors.

{ ■ + ■ = ■ } { ■ + ■ = ■ } { ■ + ■ = ■ }

TERTIARY ▸ RED-VIOLET | RED-ORANGE | YELLOW-ORANGE | YELLOW-GREEN | BLUE-GREEN | BLUE-VIOLET

Created through the combination of one primary hue and one secondary hue either equally or unequally.

ACHROMATIC ▸ WHITE | GRAY | BLACK

Meaning without color, neutral.

/color wheel/

12-spoke wheel that comprises three groups of colors: primary (three), secondary (three), and tertiary (six). The wheel is a visual organization of all hues according to their chromatic relationship.

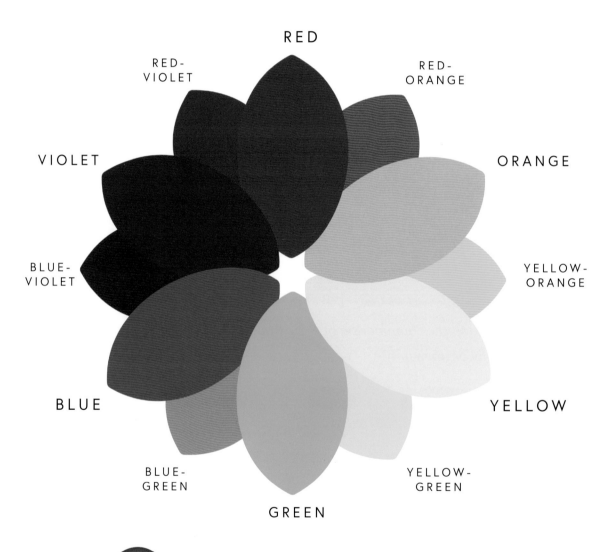

RED

RED-VIOLET

RED-ORANGE

VIOLET

ORANGE

BLUE-VIOLET

YELLOW-ORANGE

BLUE

YELLOW

BLUE-GREEN

YELLOW-GREEN

GREEN

NEUTRAL: BLACK, GRAY, WHITE

Color Psychology and Vision

The color wheel can be divided into two temperature zones: warm and cool. Each color's temperature elicits associated emotional responses, and the psychological effect of color is generally the same for all people. However, color preference, emotional impact and overall meaning vary between each person.

WARM COLORS ▶ RED | ORANGE | YELLOW

All hues on the color wheel that range from red to yellow.

general emotions ❯ *energy, happiness, cheer*

Design Note: Warm hues project out from a design, appearing to advance.

COOL COLORS ▶ GREEN | BLUE | VIOLET

All hues on the color wheel that range from green to violet.

general emotions ❯ *calm, restful, sad, melancholy*

Design Note: Cool hues blend into the background, appearing to recede.

In the field of floral design, it is important to recognize color associations with seasons, holidays, special occasions and symbols. Traditional color combinations for these events and occasions impact the meaning or message of a floral arrangement. For example, in the United States, the Valentine's Day holiday is represented with the floral color story of pink, red and white while the Fourth of July holiday is represented with red, white and blue flowers.

 ▶ **DESIGN TIP**

A blend of warm and cool hues in an arrangement creates depth within the design. Depth is created when warm colors advance and cool colors recede.

DESIGNER/PHOTOGRAPHER: Floral Art LA
RECIPE: *Phormium tenax, Cordyline terminalis*
"Variegated *Phormium* leaves offer the opportunity to create abstract 'weave' patterns
within thin glass paneled vases. This is accomplished by creating horizontal and vertical
stripes of leaves that intersect. Green *Cordyline* leaves provide a backing to the *Phormium*,
which holds them in place."

COLOR TERMINOLOGY

HUE ▶ *A pure color without the addition of a neutral. (white, gray, black).*
A synonym for color.

TINT ▶ *A pure hue with added white. Example: Pink is a tint of red.*

SHADE ▶ *A pure hue with added black. Example: Burgundy is a shade of red.*

TONE ▶ *A pure hue with added gray. Example: Dusty pink is a tone of red.*

VALUE ▶ *The lightness or darkness of a hue determined by the amount of neutrals*
(white, gray, black) added.

CHROMA ▶ *The intensity of a hue based on the brightness or dullness as a result*
of the amount of gray. The degree of vividness or saturation of a hue.

DESIGN TIP ◀

Note that memorizing color schemes is less important than understanding how colors interact with each other in an arrangement to develop meaning. Color stories assist artisans in evoking a particular mood, defining substance and identifying value for the viewer.

COLOR SCHEMES

MONOCHROMATIC ▸ *A single pure hue and any or all of its tints, tones and shades.*

ANALOGOUS ▸ *Adjacent hues on the color wheel, including one primary hue, that form a 90-degree angle (one-fourth of the color wheel; three hues on the 12-spoke color wheel).*

COMPLEMENTARY ▸ *Two hues (and/or their tints, tones and shades) that lie directly opposite each other on the color wheel.*

SPLIT COMPLEMENTARY ▸ *One hue and the two hues adjacent to its direct complement on the color wheel (and/or their tints, tones and shades).*

TRIADIC ▸ *Three hues (and/or their tints, tones and shades) that are equidistant from each other on the color wheel. These will be either the three primary colors, three secondary colors or three tertiary colors.*

POLYCHROMATIC ▸ *Any combination of colors. A synonym for multicolored.*

ANACHROMATIC ▸ *A combination of the neutrals: black, gray and white.*

TETRADIC ▸ *Four hues (and/or their tints, tones and shades) equally spaced on the color wheel. This harmony will always comprise one primary, one secondary and two tertiary colors.*

COLOR SCHEMES

DIADIC ▸ *Two colors that are two colors apart on the 12-spoke color wheel.*

ALTERNATE COMPLEMENTARY ▸ *A triad of hues and a direct complement of one of the three hues in the triad.*

FULL COMPLEMENTARY ▸ *One hue, its direct complement and the two hues adjacent to that direct complement.*

NEAR COMPLEMENTARY ▸ *One hue and one of the two hues adjacent to its direct complement.*

ANALOGOUS COMPLEMENTARY ▸ *An analogous color scheme and the one hue directly opposite the middle color in the analogous color scheme.*

DOUBLE COMPLEMENTARY ▸ *Two pairs of complementary colors. They may or may not be adjacent to each other on the color wheel.*

DOUBLE SPLIT COMPLEMENTARY ▸ *Two pairs of complementary colors that lie on both sides of any single pair of complementary colors (forming an "X" across the color wheel).*

FORM
[element]

The floral design term *form* is synonymous with the word *shape*.

Forms in floral design are identified in two ways:

> 1. *the individual components, or media, that make up a floral arrangement (flowers, foliage, container)*
>
> 2. *the overall shape of the floral arrangement (round, oval, square, rectangle, triangle)*

Form by Medium Within a Composition

When referring to form as the individual shapes of flowers, foliages and containers, we can categorize them by their individual contours. The various forms of flowers and foliage can be grouped into four distinct categories: line, mass, filler and form.

DESIGNER/PHOTOGRAPHER: Lori McNorton
RECIPE: *Chamelaucium uncinatum, Eustoma grandiflorum, Lilium* spp., *Liriope* spp., *Pittosporum tobira, Rosa* spp., *Ruscus aculeatus*
"The combination of fresh cut flowers, assorted foliage and blooming branches, such as *Rosa, Lilium, Eustoma, Chamelaucium, Liriope, Pittosporum* and *Ruscus* make for a stunning springtime arrangement that comprises of all four flower forms"

(opposite page)
DESIGNER: Laura Dowling
RECIPE: *Antirrhinum* spp., *Dianthus caryophyllus, Hyacinthus orientalis, Jasminum* spp.,
Myrtus communis, Pelargonium spp., *Ranunculus asiaticus, Rosa* spp.
"A profusion of pink blossoms, including *Rosa, Hydrangea, Antirrhinum, Ranunculus* and *Jasminum*, in a classic oval shape, is evocative of spring."
PHOTOGRAPHER: Kevin Allen

Gladiolus grandiflorus

BOTANICAL FORM ▸ LINE

Materials that have a clear linear quality about them. They are typically tall and thin and help create the framework or primary lines in a design.

examples ❯ *Antirrhinum majus, Delphinium elatum, Gladiolus grandiflorus, Liatris spicata, Moluccella laevis, Polianthes tuberosa, Xerophyllum tenax*

Gerbera jamesonii

BOTANICAL FORM ▸ MASS

Botanicals that are typically round and full, most often with only a single flower to a stem. They are used as focal points in many design styles while also providing volume and positive space.

examples ❯ *Achillea filipendulina, Anemone coronaria, Centaurea cyanus, Gerbera jamesonii, Paeonia lactiflora, Ranunculus asiaticus*

Chamelaucium uncinatum

BOTANICAL FORM ▶ FILLER

Characterized by small flowers, leaves, buds, or seed pods in large quantities on a single stem. They are used to fill spaces and connect flower placements in order to develop a design's unity.

examples ❯ *Acacia baileyana, Chamelaucium uncinatum, Bupleurum griffithii, Hypericum androsaemum, Limonium latifolium, Solidago serotina*

Iris spp.

BOTANICAL FORM ▶ FORM

Flowers and foliages that have unusual and distinctive shapes. These botanicals typically attract more attention than other types and are often featured at the focal point of a design.

examples ❯ *Alpinia purpurata, Ananas comosus, Anthurium* spp., *Celosia cristata, Nelumbo nucifera, Strelitzia reginae, Iris* spp.

DESIGN TIP

The combination of forms within an arrangement gives interest to the composition.

DESIGNER: Françoise Weeks
RECIPE: *Clematis* spp., *Lathyrus odoratus*, *Alchemilla* spp., *Gloriosa* spp. (buds), *Ruta graveolens*, *Allium spirale*, *Rubus fruticosus*, *Echeveria* spp., *Papaver* spp. (seed pods), *Physalis* spp.
PHOTOGRAPHER: Joni Shimabukuro

DESIGNER: Laura Dowling
RECIPE: *Dahlia* spp., *Cordyline fruticosa, Hypericum perforatum, Ruscus aculeatus*
"A crescent bouquet of black *Dahlia,* Italian *Ruscus* and purple *Cordyline* leaves is a study in line and form."
PHOTOGRAPHER: Kevin Allen

Warning!

This may be slightly confusing at first because the term *form* has three different meanings in floral design.

1. **Form** is the individual shape of each medium (botanicals and containers).

2. **Form** is a particular shape of a flower that is distinctive in character.

3. **Form** is the overall shape of the constructed floral arrangement.

Form by Composition

The individual forms of materials (flowers, foliage, and container) assembled together create a shape – also referred to as a form. Form, in this case, refers to either the outline or the three-dimensional shape of an arrangement, and the placement of the botanicals within the arrangement creates this overall form.

Photo: Justin Parker

Designer: Nancy Teasley/Oak & the Owl
Recipe: *Lilium* spp.
"Using low-temp glue, I glued *Lilium* blooms, one inside another, to create a garland around the back of a ghost chair.
After the event, the glue popped right off the plastic chair without marring it."

The most recognizable floral arrangement forms are geometric shapes. The circle's influence can be seen in round, oval, crescent-shaped and Hogarth-curve designs. A triangular floral design can be symmetrical or asymmetrical. A static line arrangement may be vertical, horizontal or diagonal. In the "Styles of Floral Design" section of this book *(Pages 66-87)*, we will take a closer look at the various forms that can be created with floral arrangements.

(opposite page)
Designer/Photographer: Floral Art LA
Recipe: *Zantedeschia aethiopica, Phalaenopsis amabilis, Monstera deliciosa, Xanthorrhoea johnsonii*
"This arrangement features an architectural 'hedge' of *Xanthorrhoea* grass accented with textured green *Monstera* leaves and lush clusters of *Zantedeschia* and *Phalaenopsis*. It is both modern and long lasting."

OPEN FORMS

▸ *A light and airy floral arrangement where negative space is present.*

▸ *The overall aesthetic of the design is whimsical.*

▸ *Geometric shapes are implied by a general outline of materials.*

CLOSED FORMS

▸ *A dense arrangement of botanicals where little to no negative space is incorporated.*

▸ *The overall aesthetic of the design is full and usually compact.*

▸ *Geometric shapes are formed by dense outlines.*

FRAGRANCE
[element]

Compared to other artistic practices, botanical arrangements are different in that they feature a medium that is scented. The fact that flowers and foliage appeal to our olfactory sense is a remarkable attribute to floral design. It heightens our experience with the arrangements, linking them to memory. However, it is important to note that not all floral arrangements will contain a high fragrance element, and depending on the setting, fragrance could be a detriment to the display due to allergies, distaste, or competing aromas such as food.

Examples of Fragrant Botanicals

{ ▶ *Botanical Species* ❯ *fragrance attributes* }

▶ *Abies spp.* ❯ *pine, tangerine*

▶ *Allium spp.* ❯ *onion, spicy*

▶ *Buxus sempervirens* ❯ *cat urine*

▶ *Chrysanthemum spp.* ❯ *earthy, herb-like*

▶ *Dianthus spp.* ❯ *peppery, clove*

▶ *Eucalyptus spp.* ❯ *minty, honey*

▶ *Freesia corymbosa* ❯ *sweet, peppery*

▶ *Gardenia jasminoides* ❯ *heady, sultry, jasmine-like*

▶ *Gypsophila elegans* ❯ *stinky feet*

▶ *Hyacinthus orientalis* ❯ *sweet, intoxicating*

▶ *Matthiola incana* ❯ *peppery, spicy*

▶ *Myrtus communis* ❯ *balmy, green*

▶ *Paeonia spp.* ❯ *fresh, floral, mild*

▶ *Polianthes tuberosa* ❯ *heady, sultry, jasmine-like*

▶ *Rosa spp.* ❯ *honey, green tea, moss*

▶ *Stephanotis floribunda* ❯ *sweet, honey*

▶ *Syringa vulgaris* ❯ *spring, fresh, heady*

▶ *Tagetes spp.* ❯ *spicy, musty, strong*

DESIGNER: The Flori.Culture
RECIPE: *Craspedia globosa, Leucospermum* spp., *Liriope muscari, Narcissus* spp., *Ranunculus asiaticus, Rhapidophyllum hystrix*
"We created this modern palm-frond trough for a contemporary magazine photo shoot. To create this look, we cut fronds into circular shapes and arranged them into a clear-tape-gridded trough and then set a large asymmetrical accent on the horizontal line to create a focal point with vibrant sunset-hued blossoms."
PHOTOGRAPHER: Amber Snow

LINE
[element]

Line is the visual path within a floral arrangement that the viewers' eyes follow and that creates both movement and structure within the design.

Lines within designs are built in two ways:

1. by the placement of "line" form botanicals and/or

2. the progression of botanicals in sizes from small to large or from bud to full bloom.

In essence, each line creates the skeletal pattern, framework or three-dimensional form of an arrangement.

Each line classification evokes a particular mood or feeling based on the movement of the viewers' eyes within an arrangement. Furthermore, lines can be categorized based on their static or dynamic characteristics. Vertical and horizontal lines are considered static due to the lack of movement they create; they can appear to be regimented and motionless. In comparison, diagonal and curved lines are considered dynamic; they give floral designs movement, energy, and vibrancy.

Classification of Lines

▶ *STATIC:* *lack of movement, regimented and motionless*

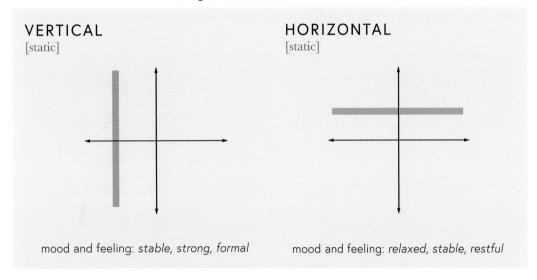

VERTICAL
[static]

mood and feeling: *stable, strong, formal*

HORIZONTAL
[static]

mood and feeling: *relaxed, stable, restful*

▶ *DYNAMIC:* *creates movement, shifting and advancing*

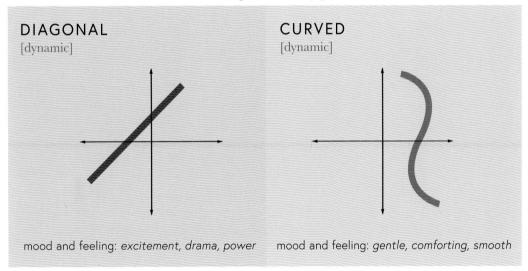

DIAGONAL
[dynamic]

mood and feeling: *excitement, drama, power*

CURVED
[dynamic]

mood and feeling: *gentle, comforting, smooth*

▶ **DESIGN TIP**

When a static line and a dynamic line are combined in a design (such as a vertical line intersected by a diagonal line), the resulting lines of opposition provide heightened visual interest.

SIZE
[element]

Size is determined by dimensions. When designing an arrangement, it is important to consider the selection of compatible botanicals and vessel based on size. Furthermore, size conveys perceived value in an arrangement; large arrangements are often considered more valuable than smaller arrangements although this is not always accurate.

Warning!

In floral design, size applies the elements of line, form and space combined to determine the arrangement's measurement. Note that because size applies other elements to determine the measurement, size is sometimes not considered a true element, by definition.

SPACE
[element]

Space refers to the three-dimensional area between and around the materials within a design as well as the areas those materials occupy. In floral design, positive space and negative space are assigned to areas that contain materials or are without materials.

POSITIVE SPACE

▸ *The area within a composition that is **occupied** by materials.*

▸ *Within an arrangement, each botanical occupies a specific area.*

▸ *A completed flower arrangement occupies a specific area within a room.*

NEGATIVE SPACE

▸ *The empty or open area **between** materials or an area **devoid** of materials.*

▸ *The empty areas make the materials occupying positive space appear greater in prominence and distinctiveness within the design.*

DESIGN TIP

Proper placement of positive or negative space within a floral arrangement may draw the viewers' eyes to the focal point as well as create depth to an arrangement.

(opposite page, top)
DESIGNER: The Flori.Culture
RECIPE: *Rosa* spp., *Tagetes erecta*
"We created these cocktail table arrangements for a Day of the Dead-themed event. The sizes of the *Rosa* and *Tagetes* blossoms are about 3 inches in diameter, which creates fabulous proportions when designing in the 5-inch-diameter vessel."
PHOTOGRAPHER: Macey Sierka

(opposite page, bottom)
DESIGNERS: Natasha Lisitsa and Daniel Schultz
RECIPE: *Anthurium andraeanum, Arctostaphylos manzanita, Forsythia suspensa, Salix matsudana*
"A radiant central composition of yellow *Forsythia* and red *Arctostaphylos* branches alludes to the sun and earth, the combined vital energy common to us all. Orbiting this form is an ascending spiral, which presents allusions to the building blocks of nature: the earth orbiting the sun, the atom, DNA and the continuous path of life along which we all travel."
PHOTOGRAPHER: Erin Beach

TEXTURE
[element]

Texture refers to the physical surface quality of a material within a floral design (botanical, vessel, accessory). Texture can be either tactile (noticeable to the touch), visual (noticeable to the eye) or both. Some materials have more than one texture, such the velvety petals of *Rosa* spp. hybrids with jagged prickles or a smooth *Anthurium* spathe with a bumpy spadix.

Note that distance affects the importance of texture within a design. The closer the viewer is to a design, the more noticeable the details of texture become. Thus, texture becomes less of a consideration the farther away an arrangement is viewed because it may be unnoticeable (such as on a stage or altar when viewed from an audience).

DESIGN TIP

When designing an arrangement, incorporating a variety of textures will increase visual interest. However, using too many varied textures may detract from the arrangement. Balance is key!

(above)
DESIGNER: The Flori.Culture
RECIPE: *Astilbe* spp., *Cymbidium* spp., *Dahlia* spp., *Matthiola incana*, *Nephrolepis exaltata*, *Opuntia* spp., *Scabiosa atropurpurea*
"Certainly this floral arrangement has some texture. A variety of textures is juxtaposed to create high impact in the design. The spiky *Opuntia* with the slick *Cymbidium* makes this design funky yet sophisticated in the mercury-glass vessel."
PHOTOGRAPHER: Macey Sierka

(right)
DESIGNER: The Flori.Culture
RECIPE: *Colocasia esculenta*
"Tropical arrangements have a tendency to look harsh and jagged in texture. However, this tropical foliage, *Colocasia esculenta*, has a smooth velvety surface that can create contrast to rough textures in many designs. At The Flori.Culture, we love these leaves so much that we create monobotanical arrangements with them to show off their textural distinctiveness."
PHOTOGRAPHER: Macey Sierka

Botanical Texture Examples

{ ▸ *Botanical Species* ❯ *texture* }

▸ *Adiantum capillus-veneris* ❯ *feathery, light*

▸ *Centaurea cineraria* ❯ *fuzzy, thick, velvety*

▸ *Echinops bannaticus* ❯ *barbed, harsh*

▸ *Heliconia stricta* ❯ *glossy, finished, firm*

▸ *Helleborus orientalis* ❯ *pleated, glossy, sculptured*

▸ *Papaver nudicaule* ❯ *fragile, papery*

▸ *Picea abies* ❯ *inflexible, prickly, sharp*

▸ *Scabiosa stellata* ❯ *crispy, scratchy*

▸ *Syringa vulgaris* ❯ *dense, fluffy, soft*

▸ *Xerochrysum bracteatum* ❯ *coarse, blistered*

DESIGN TIP

Advanced color schemes – such as polychromatic or tetradic – enhance the visual quality of textures in comparison to monochromatic designs, in which texture becomes less prominent.

PRINCIPLES OF DESIGN

Balance, Dominance, Harmony, Proportion, Scale, Rhythm, Unity

The principles of design are the fundamental guidelines in the creation of art. They assist the designer in steering the organization of botanical materials into a harmonious arrangement. Each principle is a design theory and is applied through the use of the elements of design. For example, well-achieved line (element) in an arrangement can create symmetrical or asymmetrical balance (principle).

DESIGNER: The Flori.Culture
RECIPE: *Antirrhinum majus, Bougainvillea glabra, Elaeagnus angustifolia, Moluccella laevis, Olea europaea, Passiflora incarnata, Rosa* spp.
"This gathered bouquet was created to showcase asymmetry. Not only does the *Passiflora incarnata* drape on the right side of the design but the *Rosa* spp. and *Bougainvillea glabra* also are placed to highlight asymmetrical placement within the center of the design."
PHOTOGRAPHER: Brealyn Nenes

BALANCE
[primary principle]

Balance is determined by the overall stability of a floral design. Within a botanical arrangement, balance is created by methodical placements of materials as either symmetrical or asymmetrical.

DESIGNER: The Flori.Culture
RECIPE: *Muscari armeniacum, Viola tricolor*
"In this vase series, balance is formed through the use of symmetrical placement of high and low clear glass bottles filled with uniform placement of *Muscari armeniacum* accented with *Viola tricolor.*"
PHOTOGRAPHER: Macey Sierka

DESIGNER: The Flori.Culture
RECIPE: *Tillandsia xerographica, Tulipa* spp.
"The Flori.Culture frequently designs in asymmetrical balance because the designers view asymmetry as more visually stimulating. Asymmetry allows the designer to enhance the element of line in the arrangement. Sometimes all it takes is an accent, like this *Tillandsia xerographica.*"
PHOTOGRAPHER: Macey Sierka

SYMMETRICAL BALANCE

▸ *Formal, dignified, strong*

▸ *Appears man-made*

▸ *Mirror image on both sides of axis*

ASYMMETRICAL BALANCE

▸ *Appears natural*

▸ *Imperfect symmetry*

▸ *Different on either side of axis*

Physical or Mechanical Balance
The actual distribution of weight (materials) within a botanical arrangement. When physical balance is achieved, a floral design will stand stably on its own whether the design is visually asymmetrical or symmetrical.

Visual Balance
The visual perception that an arrangement is physically balanced and stable. When an arrangement appears to be unstable, it is visually disturbing. (A person may find him/herself tilting his/her head to the side to straighten the arrangement.)

DESIGN TIP

Although a design may be asymmetrical, visual balance can be created with varying sizes, colors and textures of materials. Heavy-looking materials are generally dark or bright in color; large or mass in form; and coarse, rough or shiny in texture. Heavy-looking materials are generally dark or bright in color, large or mass in form, and coarse or shiny in texture.

DOMINANCE
[primary principle]

Dominance is the visual organization of materials emphasizing one or more areas within the arrangement. Essentially, the elements are used to draw attention to a certain component, or multiple components, of the arrangement. Furthermore, individual materials may exhibit dominance due to their intrinsic characteristics or may be developed as a center of interest in a design to create a theme or mood.

DESIGNER: AZ Petal Pusher
RECIPE: *Dypsis lutescens, Hippeastrum spp., Hydrangea macrophylla, Monstera deliciosa, Phalaenopsis amabilis, Zantedeschia aethiopica*
"This arrangement takes on a naturalistic design form using linear *Zantedeschia* stems to create a base while massing the white florals and tropical leaves at the top."
PHOTOGRAPHER: Hannah Costello Photography

EMPHASIS

▸ *An area in a composition that conveys importance to make it stand out.*

▸ *Emphasis is created through strategic placement of materials to highlight the **focal point** and **accent(s)** within a design.*

FOCAL POINT

▸ *Area(s) of greatest visual impact within a design.*

▸ *The focal point is determined by the linear origin of convergence, where the eyes are drawn.*

ACCENT

▸ *Supplemental detail added to a design to enhance interest.*

▸ *Accents may be materials that are associated with the focal area(s) or overall theme.*

DESIGN TIP

Individual botanical materials themselves (such as form flowers) can exhibit dominance due to their intrinsic characteristics. Or, designers can develop dominance by emphasizing a focal point or accents to act as a center of interest in a design and to create a theme or mood.

HARMONY
[primary principle]

Harmony refers to the aesthetic quality created by the careful selection and placement of materials within a botanical composition. It is the result of a pleasing combination of the elements and correct application of the principles. When all components of an arrangement (flowers, foliage, container, accessories, etc.) blend well and are suitable for the design's intended purpose, harmony is achieved.

Harmony is both intangible and tangible. Intangibly, harmony demonstrates the artist's implied theme and mood of an arrangement. Tangibly, it relates to the correct assimilation of the elements of design. Because of this intangible and tangible nature, the principle of harmony is based on the viewer's personal opinion and taste. In other words, what may be a harmonious arrangement to you may not be to another person.

DESIGN TIP

Know thy audience! For the designer, it is critical to know the taste of the recipient or theme of the event in order to design a harmonious arrangement for the client. To do so, it is important to evaluate the application of the elements and principles as well as the choice of materials in the composition.

PROPORTION
[primary principle]

Proportion refers to the comparative size relationship between parts of a floral arrangement. In other words, proportion is determining how the size and quantity of botanical materials within the composition relate and associate with each other as a whole in the floral design.

DESIGNER: Pigsty Studio
RECIPE: *Allium giganteum, Amaryllis belladonna., Anthurium andraeanum, Cotinus coggygria, Polystichum munitum, Rosa* spp.
"The dark lavender-violet *Allium* complements the deep purple *Cotinus* and spathe of the variegated *Anthurium*. Using the pink tropicals, we incorporated varieties of *Rosa* in apricot and peach for grounding within the hand-held bouquet design."
PHOTOGRAPHER: Hope Sword

SIZE AND PROPORTION

▸ *The size, quantity and length of each botanical material selected to be combined together in a design must be proportionate to each other.*

▸ *The size, quantity and length of the botanicals also dictate the proportions of the container based on size.*

GOLDEN RATIO

The generally recommended height proportion of botanicals to container is 1.5 to 2 times the height and/or width of the container (above or to the sides of the container's opening edge).

DESIGN TIP

A frequently recommended proportion for botanical materials is:

▸ 65 percent small size or cool color
▸ 25 percent moderate size or warm/cool color
▸ 10 percent large size or warm color

DESIGNER: Laura Dowling
RECIPE: *Dianthus caryophyllus, Rosa* spp. and pink tissue paper folded to look like *Cyclamen persicum*
"Multiple bouquets of fuchsia-hued flowers are arranged in the sculpted and symmetrical Georgian style."
PHOTOGRAPHER: Kevin Allen

DESIGN TIP

The height of a floral arrangement for a table setting should be considered beforehand to allow for guests' conversation. The general rule is a floral arrangement height limit of 12-14 inches.

[A room with high ceilings may require a taller arrangement(s).]

SCALE
[secondary principle]

Scale is the ratio of the size of a botanical composition to the surrounding environment where it will be displayed. When determining the size of an arrangement, consider the size of the setting. What are the dimensions of the room? What is the size of the table/altar/shelf? Obtaining the measurements of these areas is essential to identifying the overall size of the arrangement so that it is proportionate to its environment.

Warning!

Do not confuse the definition of scale with proportion. Proportion addresses the size relationship between botanicals within a floral arrangement while scale addresses the size relationship between the arrangement placement and its environment.

RHYTHM

[primary principle]

Rhythm is the visual journey within an arrangement created by elements of design. It is the flow of a viewer's eyes from the focal point to the edges of the arrangement and back again. Rhythm can be achieved in several ways, including the secondary principles of depth, repetition and transition.

DEPTH

▶ *The placement of materials at different levels, or planes, to create a three-dimensional effect within an arrangement.*

REPETITION

▶ *The repeating of like elements or materials within a botanical composition.*

▶ *Repetition creates **patterns** within an arrangement.*

TRANSITION

▶ *The abrupt or gradual change in materials or elements within a design.*

▶ *The terms **sequencing** and **gradation** describe this technique of placing materials in a gradual and systematic sequence of change.*

DESIGNER: The Flori.Culture
RECIPE: *Asparagus setaceus, Aspidistra elatior, Nephrolepis exaltata, Polystichum munitum, Paeonia* spp.
"In this design, the visual rhythmic path flows from the focal point of the *Paeonia* spp. and curled *Aspidistra elatior* to the *Asparagus setaceus* on the top right of the arrangement."
PHOTOGRAPHER: Macey Sierka

DESIGN TIP

Think of rhythm in a floral arrangement as synonymous to a song. Do the materials flow together in a pattern to evoke a mood or theme, and thus, is the arrangement harmonious?

DESIGNER: Isari Flower Studio
RECIPE: *Antirrhinum majus, Dahlia* spp., *Hippeastrum* spp., *Phalaenopsis* spp., *Phytolacca decandra, Rosa* spp.
"Unity is combining color and texture cohesively. This arrangement is constructed with tighter
(not organic) blooms and a monochromatic color scheme, which creates the unity."
PHOTOGRAPHER: Shane and Lauren Photography

UNITY

[primary principle]

Unity is the cohesive relationship of the individual botanical materials and the elements in a design to each other. In other words, unity is the sum of the parts of the arrangement that gives purpose, style and spirit to the design. It is achieved only when all of the principles and elements of design are well executed. Note that an important aspect of unity is that the whole composition must be more important than its individual botanical materials.

Warning!
Do not confuse the definition of unity with harmony. Unity refers to the relationship of materials as a cohesive unit while harmony refers to the viewer's aesthetic opinion of the design.

DESIGN TIP

Unity is lacking in arrangements that can be "divided" into sections. This can be avoided when a designer initially sees a floral design as a single cohesive unit and not as a combination of parts.

PILLOWING

TECHNIQUES FOR BUILDING ARRANGEMENTS

/technique/

the method of procedure and use of skill to render an artistic work.
Techniques are used to create a floral design composition;
they are the skill sets required to complete an artistic work.

Practicing and honing these established floral design techniques to create floral styles *(Pages 66-87)* assists designers in the practice of creating meaningful and well-constructed botanical artworks.

(above and opposite page)
DESIGNER: The Flori.Culture | PHOTOGRAPHER: Macey Sierka

▶ *ARMATURE*

An armature is a supportive frame or grid within an arrangement. The frame can be built from organic or nonorganic materials. An armature can be functional, decorative or both.

RECIPE: *Jasminum sambac, Olea europaea, Rubus idaeus, Salix matsudana, Viburnum opulus*

TECHNIQUE: *Salix matsudana* branches are tied together with paper-covered wire to create an structure within which botanical materials can be intertwined, for a lush garden aesthetic.

RECIPE: *Rhapidophyllum hystrix*

▶ *BALING*

Baling consists of gathering, massing, tying and compressing cut plant materials together to create a definable geometric shape (circle, square, rectangle). Plant material is held together using a variety of materials (organic or nonorganic). It is a combination of several design techniques (including stacking, binding, wrapping).

TECHNIQUE: Each palm frond is placed one upon another in a layered radiating circle. The fronds are secured together with decorative silver wire wrapped at the center point around each frond.

▶ *BANDING*

Banding is a purely aesthetic technique that serves no functional purpose. A group of stems, decorative objects, or a container may be banded for ornamentation.

RECIPE: *Anemone coronaria, Echeveria* spp., *Eryngium amethystinum, Hydrangea macrophylla, Pieris japonica, Jacobaea maritima*

TECHNIQUE: This cylindrical vessel is embellished with a watercolor-painted canvas band for decoration.

DESIGN TIP

Materials used to bind or band may include botanicals, raffia, ribbon, thread, wire, yarn, fabric and tape.

▶ *BINDING*

Binding is a mechanical, functional process of tying materials together into units and holding items in place to create stability. The functional material holding the materials in place also could be decorative.

RECIPE: *Eucalyptus* spp., *Laurus nobilis*

TECHNIQUE: A foliage garland of *Eucalyptus* spp. and *Laurus nobilis* is secured together with paper-covered wire around each stem or collection of stems.

(above and opposite page)
DESIGNER: The Flori.Culture | PHOTOGRAPHER: Macey Sierka

▶ *BUNCHING*

Bunching is a time-saving method of incorporating a collection (gathered or bound together) of stems, of the same genus and species, into an arrangement with only one insertion. This functional practice tends to be utilized with small-stemmed materials. Several collections of stems can be inserted next to each other.

RECIPE: *Diospyros virginiana, Helianthus annuus, Pieris japonica, Rosa canina, Xanthorrhoea johnsonii*

TECHNIQUE: This hedge arrangement is created by inserting several small groupings of *Xanthorrhoea johnsonii* into OASIS® Floral Foam Maxlife. The top of the *Xanthorrhoea johnsonii* is trimmed in a straight line to accentuate the hedge aesthetic.

▶ *BUNDLING*

Bundling involves placing fresh-cut or dried flower stems together in radiating symmetry above and below a single binding point. The bundle can be placed either vertically or horizontally within a design or to create the overall form.

RECIPE: *Anemone coronaria, Callistephus chinensis, Centaurea cyanus, Crocosmia × crocosmiiflora, Dahlia* spp., *Lavandula* spp.

TECHNIQUE: Peruvian pottery is set with OASIS® Floral Foam Maxlife, then a bundle of *Lavandula* spp. is secured with both twine and a pin of floral wire into the floral foam. The remaining ingredients are placed around the bundle but allowing the *Lavandula* spp. blooms and stems to still be showcased in the design.

(above and opposite page)
DESIGNER: The Flori.Culture | PHOTOGRAPHER: Macey Sierka

RECIPE: *Celosia cristata, Dianthus barbatus, Dianthus caryophyllus*

TECHNIQUE: In this sculpted container, each individual flower type – *Celosia cristata, Dianthus barbatus* and *Dianthus caryophyllus* – are grouped together but placed so that the identity of each flower type's petals blend together.

▶ CLUSTERING

Clustering is the grouping of the same types of botanicals adjacent to one another so that the identity and quantity of the individual stems is indistinguishable. The cluster in the design functions as a single unit. This is different from grouping, where materials retain their own identities. Certain types of botanicals blend better together than others; flowers with defined centers do not create the desired look.

▶ DETAILING

Detailing involves precisely placing materials to complete, accent, or add interest to an area or areas of a floral arrangement.

RECIPE: *Rosa* spp.

TECHNIQUE: A composite flower is created by adding petals to the outer layer of a single full-bloomed flower to add interest and enlarge the apparent size of the blossom.

▶ *ENCLOSURE*

Designing an arrangement to be confined "within" a space/object. The techniques of veiling and sheltering may be applied.

RECIPE: *Jasminum sambac, Scabiosa* spp., *Serruria florida*

TECHNIQUE: Within the glass lantern, the vines are arranged at the base in OASIS® Floral Foam Maxlife to create a greenhouse aesthetic for the botanicals growing out of their enclosure.

(above and opposite page)
DESIGNER: The Flori.Culture | PHOTOGRAPHER: Macey Sierka

▶ *FACING*

Facing is the strategic placement of two or more botanicals (flower "faces"/ leaves) positioned in the same or opposite direction of each another. Positioning this way creates a statement as well as increases interest. To achieve emphasis and unity, face botanicals toward one another. To achieve the feeling of rejection, face botanicals away from one another.

RECIPE: *Monstera deliciosa, Viola tricolor*

TECHNIQUE: Large *Monstera deliciosa* leaves are placed into two emerald-green vessels to face each other; the technique is accentuated by adhering *Viola tricolor* to the larger leaves with florist wire.

(above and opposite page)
DESIGNER: The Flori.Culture | PHOTOGRAPHER: Macey Sierka

RECIPE: *Cymbidium* spp., *Echeveria* spp., *Olea europaea, Prunus armeniaca*

▶ *FRAMING*

Framing involves forming an outline or boundary of the arrangement on one or more sides using linear botanicals to encompass, isolate, contain, showcase or call attention to the framed area. Framing focuses the viewers' eyes by directing them to the focal point. Placement extends from the sides and rises above the central materials.

TECHNIQUE: *Cymbidium* spp., *Echeveria* spp. and *Prunus armeniaca* are set within the metallic gold vase using the pavé technique, with branches of *Olea europaea* rising from the vase to frame the pavéd botanicals below.

RECIPE: *Anthurium andraeanum, Aspidistra elatior, Paeonia* spp., *Ranunculus asiaticus, Rosa rugosa, Tulipa* spp.

▶ *GROUPING*

Grouping is placing the same types of botanicals together with negative space between each botanical group; this allows for the individual characteristics of each flower type to remain evident. Grouping emphasizes each botanical used based on its individual form, color and texture.

TECHNIQUE: Each flower type is grouped within the arrangement; however, the element of negative space is exaggerated by ensuring that each flower type has ample space between another.

▸ *HAND TYING*

Hand tying is a method of arranging botanicals in one's hands with diagonally crossed stems. One hand holds the bouquet while the other adds stems. The stems are bound where they cross with any type of binding material. Bouquet forms are usually round or oval.

RECIPE: *Chamelaucium* spp., *Delphinium* spp., *Echinacea* spp., *Eucalyptus* spp., *Lavandula* spp., *Paeonia* spp.

TECHNIQUE: Each stem is stripped of foliage below the hand while each stem placement in the hand is diagonally set to create an interlocking system. To finish the design, the stems are wrapped with tape and/or ribbon at their binding point.

(above and opposite page)
DESIGNER: The Flori.Culture | PHOTOGRAPHER: Macey Sierka

▸ *KUBARI*

Kubari originates from Japanese ikebana. It is the placement of botanical materials within a vessel as a support for other stems inserted into the arrangement.

RECIPE: *Calathea ornata, Dahlia* spp., *Eucomis autumnalis, Leucospermum* spp., *Moluccella laevis*

TECHNIQUE: *Moluccella laevis* form the grid within the glass vessel to create both an aesthetic quality in the arrangement as well as a structure for stabilizing the arrangement's other botanicals.

▶ *LACING*

Lacing is a method of interweaving and crossing stems to create a natural "grid" to hold flowers in position within a container.

RECIPE: *Anemone coronaria, Ranunculus asiaticus, Rosa* spp., *Tulipa* spp.

TECHNIQUE: Each stem is placed within the square vase in a grid fashion, where the stems are interwoven to hold each individual flower in place.

(above and opposite page)
DESIGNER: The Flori.Culture | PHOTOGRAPHER: Macey Sierka

▸ LAYERING

Layering is the process of arranging flat-surfaced botanicals directly on top of one another, to overlap, with no space between. The materials may be layered individually or in bound bunches or stacks.

RECIPE: *Galax urceolata*

TECHNIQUE: The *Galax urceolata* rosette is created by layering each leaf upon the other in a radiating pattern and securing the stems together with both a stapler and stem wrap.

▸ MIRRORING

Mirroring involves the placement of botanicals to create a reflection of one another and to promote symmetry within the arrangement.

RECIPE: *Rosa* spp., *Asparagus setaceus*, *Nephrolepis exaltata*, *Polystichum munitum*

TECHNIQUE: The placement of *Asparagus setaceus* and *Nephrolepis exaltata* on both sides of the vase at similar lengths and quantities creates a reflective symmetrical balance to the design in which the *Rosa* spp. are set in the center to form a pivot to the mirrored ferns.

▶ MONOBOTANICAL

A monobotanical design comprises only one type of botanical material.

RECIPE: *Gypsophila* spp.

TECHNIQUE: Only one flower type, *Gypsophila* spp., is arranged into this brass container.

▶ PAVÉ

Pavé involves the placement of botanicals on the same plane, side by side, to cover the base of a design. It creates a flat cobblestone effect.

RECIPE: *Dianthus caryophyllus*

TECHNIQUE: This pavé design was created by densely placing each *Dianthus caryophyllus* bloom next to another so that the petals are touching one another on the same dimensional plane.

(above and opposite page)
DESIGNER: The Flori.Culture | PHOTOGRAPHER: Macey Sierka

RECIPE: *Celosia argentea, Matthiola incana, Paeonia* spp., *Scabiosa* spp.

▶ *PILLOWING*

Pillowing is a specialized form of clustering in which like botanicals are arranged closely together in mounded groupings. A series of these clusters (pillows) may flow like hills and valleys, with some being larger or taller than others. By clustering materials closely together, they lose their individual identities. Each "pillow" should comprise only one type of botanical and should be a different color and texture than those next to it.

TECHNIQUE: Each type of flower is arranged into a mounded cluster (pillow), and the clusters are then arranged into a single container. The clusters may be of varying sizes and arranged at varying heights.

▶ *SEQUENCING*

Sequencing is the placement of flowers and other materials in a gradual and progressive transition of size, color or texture. Size may move from small to large or from bud to fully opened blooms; color moves from light to dark; and texture moves from smooth to coarse.

RECIPE: *Astilbe* spp., *Daucus carota, Delphinium* spp., *Chamelaucium uncinatum*

TECHNIQUE: Three square mercury-glass vessels are set next to each other, with the botanicals clustered in monobotanical bunches, transitioning in a sequence of white to blush hues.

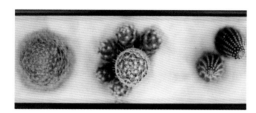

RECIPE: *Echeveria* spp.

TECHNIQUE: The trough is laid with sand at the bottom, and the root systems are cut off of the *Echeveria* spp. Each botanical is then placed on top of the sand but within the trough. The viewer can see the arrangement from both the top or sides of the vessel.

▶ *SHELTERING*

Sheltering is the placement of one or more materials, such as branches or foliage, over the design to partially enclose the underlying botanicals. The underlying material(s) remains partially visible, and the enclosed space becomes a focal point. Sheltering creates visual drama and encourages viewers to look closer to discover what is underneath.

▶ *STACKING*

Stacking is the orderly placement of like materials. The materials may be individual stems, placed in bunches, set side by side, or on top of each other, highlighting positive space.

RECIPE: *Craspedia variabilis*

TECHNIQUE: The stems of the *Craspedia variabilis* are cut off so that only the sphere remains. A needle and twine is strung to thread each bloom, stacking each on top of the other to create a lei.

(above and opposite page)
DESIGNER: The Flori.Culture | PHOTOGRAPHER: Macey Sierka

▶ TERRACING

Terracing is the arrangement of like materials in a stairstep fashion, horizontally, with negative space between each botanical type. This creates a series of levels with one material on top of another. Materials are often flat surfaced and arranged in graduated sizes.

RECIPE: *Tulipa* spp., *Asparagus setaceus, Xerophyllum tenax*

TECHNIQUE: Three gold pipe vases are set from high to low with the *Asparagus setaceus, Tulipa* spp. and *Xerophyllum tenax* spilling out of each vase in a stairstep fashion.

▶ TUFTING

Tufting involves clustering or bunching short-stemmed flowers, foliage or other materials closely together near the base of a design. The materials in each grouping should be arranged in a radiating pattern. Tufting may be used to create either an entire design or just one portion, generally at the base.

RECIPE: *Astilbe* spp., *Celosia argentea, Chamelaucium uncinatum, Dianthus* spp., *Lavandula* spp., *Lysimachia nemorum*

TECHNIQUE: Each botanical type is grouped but extends outward from the rim of the vintage coffee-can vessel to showcase each individual type's form, texture and color.

▸ *VEILING*

Veiling is the layering of light materials over more solid forms. This softens and slightly obscures the materials beneath and creates a sheer overlay effect.

RECIPE: *Anemone coronaria, Tulipa* spp.

TECHNIQUE: The feather plumes are set atop crystal candlesticks and vases to elevate the design while the *Anemone coronaria* and *Tulipa* spp. are intermingled at the base of the display to create a layered effect.

▸ *WRAPPING*

Wrapping is the covering of a single stem, a bundle of stems or an entire composition with decorative materials such as fabric, ribbon, raffia, metallic cord, thread, wire, yarn, etc. It is both functional and decorative. Wrapping also can be applied to containers to change their appearance or camouflage them.

TECHNIQUE: The stems of *Allium sphaerocephalon, Anemone coronaria* and *Astilbe* spp. are wrapped together with ribbon for both decoration and stability.

RECIPE: *Allium sphaerocephalon, Anemone coronaria, Astilbe* spp.

(above and opposite page)
DESIGNER: The Flori.Culture | PHOTOGRAPHER: Macey Sierka

▸ *ZONING*

Zoning involves placing groups of like materials in specific areas, or zones, within a composition. The negative space between each group must be ample enough so that each remains independent. This technique is often applied to a composition larger than a simple flower arrangement.

RECIPE: *Echeveria* spp.

TECHNIQUE: Three geometric terrariums create individual zones within their containers that highlight the *Echeveria* spp. This design was created by laying a shallow layer of sand in each container and cutting the *Echeveria* spp. at the base to remove the root system and soil.

STYLES OF FLORAL DESIGN

Natural, Form and Innovative

Style is a noun and a verb. It refers to the appearance of an object or an individual as well as the aesthetic process of creation. It is the way in which something is expressed or experienced by both the designer and viewer. Style is found all around us – in fashion, cuisine, dance, writing, interiors and art. Within floral design, style is portrayed by the selection of the vessels and botanicals as well as the arrangement's form, techniques applied, and the purpose or function of the design. Furthermore, the style of a botanical design evokes a certain mood or meaning for the recipient or viewer.

NATURAL STYLES

Botanical, Vegetative, Landscape

Natural-styled botanical arrangements are designed to reflect nature and the environment. These arrangements generate a whimsical, playful and eccentric vibe to their surroundings.

DESIGNER: Françoise Weeks
RECIPE: *Arctostaphylos manzanita, Anemone coronaria, Freesia corymbosa, Tulipa* spp., *Pieris japonica, Jasminum* spp., *Berzelia lanuginosa, Cornus florida, Echeveria* spp., *Hedera* spp., lichen, *Actinidia deliciosa*
PHOTOGRAPHER: Jamie Bosworth

BOTANICAL

[Style]

Designs that showcase the entire life cycle of a plant species.

This botanical style captures the life cycle of the plant, from bud formation to senescence. Botanical designs showcase the beauty of flowers without manipulation and capture their interaction within the environment. Usually, the roots/bulbs, stems, foliage and blossoms are all visible in the design.

Furthermore, botanical arrangements are constructed in a natural manner to appear as if the plants are growing. This natural growing environment is re-created at the base of the design with accents of stones, mosses, twigs and soil.

DESIGN TIP

Do not remove the blemished petals. We all strive for perfection, but within the botanical style, it is important to leave nature as intended.

(opposite page)
DESIGNER: Françoise Weeks
RECIPE: *Rosa* spp., *Galanthus nivalis, Narcissus tazetta, Muscari armeniacum, Pieris japonica, Jasminum* spp., *Brassica* spp., *Brunia albiflora, Begonia* spp., *Pelargonium* spp., *Viburnum* spp., *Echeveria* spp.
PHOTOGRAPHER: Joni Shimabukuro

VEGETATIVE
[Style]

Designs that represent plants (flowers, foliage, branches) in the habitat in which they naturally grow.

The vegetative design style is precision oriented, in which plant types are strategically selected and placed to represent a vision of nature. Within the design, the same plant species are grouped but also intermingle with other varieties to reflect their natural growth pattern.

Additionally, the height and growth angles (radial or parallel) of each plant type are reflected in the design as they would be in nature. Thought to material selection is crucial, with seasonal and geographical plant compatibility being represented.

Other materials, such as rocks, bark, moss and twigs, may be used as long as they are compatible and placed as they would be found in the environment.

DESIGNER/PHOTOGRAPHER: Floral Art LA
RECIPE: *Echeveria* spp., *Tillandsia* spp.
"Natural driftwood is adorned with clusters of rosette succulents and moss. Organic in style, this piece is ideal for semi-permanent décor or centerpieces on long rectangular tables."

DESIGN TIP
When designing this style, think of taking a photo of nature and designing the arrangement exactly to the detail showcased in the image. Think of adding soil, keeping blemishes on the plants and mimicking the curve of stems as they grow.

LANDSCAPE

[Style]

Designs that depict a large area of nature, such as a wilderness panorama or landscaped gardens.

Landscape designs represent nature in a planned manner, as humans might have cultivated it. The organization of species based on planned groupings and determined heights is critical for correct interpretation of this style. It is common in landscape designs for the plant materials to be expressed in a representational manner. For example, a *Chaenomeles lagenaria* branch might represent a tree, and a cluster of *Solidaster luteus* could represent a shrub within a design.

Furthermore, garden accents are integrated to create decorative details common in a realistic landscape (moss, rocks, bark, sand, soil, etc.).

Lastly, just as in all natural styles, the materials selected must be of the same seasonal and geographical compatibility.

DESIGNER: The Flori.Culture
RECIPE: *Echeveria* spp., *Echinacea* spp., *Serruria florida*
"To develop this design, we cut the cacti so that the root systems are no longer attached to the plant for ease of placing into a shallow container. Then, height and depth is reviewed with the placement of each *Echeveria* spp. variety (we like to group them as they grow in nature). To finish the design, we cut *Serruria florida* blooms and placed them on the cacti to look as though the plants are blooming."
PHOTOGRAPHER: Macey Sierka

DESIGN TIP

Landscape designs are generally arranged with taller materials in the back to allow the viewer a complete view of the composition.

Warning!

Do not confuse the three natural styles. Though they are similar, there are distinct differences that set them apart. Remember that a botanical style showcases all parts of a plant, a vegetative style captures a replica of undisturbed nature, and landscape style models a cultivated garden.

DESIGNER: The Flori.Culture
RECIPE: *Hippeastrum* spp., *Echinops sphaerocephalus*
"To create the triangle, one must look at the three points of the *Hippeastrum* spp. The positive space in the center of the design allows the viewer to see the triangle form a bit more clearly than negative-space triangles."
PHOTOGRAPHER: Macey Sierka

FORM STYLES
Circular, Triangular, Fan, Line

Form styles are floral arrangements defined by a geometric shape. They are composed with strategic placement of botanicals to create a particular form and may be either hand-held designs or displayed within a vessel. Within the design shapes, materials technically should not extend out of the geometric lines. Note, however, that some form sub-styles are derived from realistic forms but take on an individual personality.

CIRCULAR FORM
[Style]

Circular floral arrangements depict the form of a sphere. The materials are placed symmetrically and strategically to radiate from a central point within the design. Within the round shape, the materials may be massed to produce positive space or arranged airily to showcase negative space. This style is very versatile and is commonly used in centerpiece tablescape décor as well as bridal bouquets. Not only is it versatile in display, its construction adaptability allows for many sub-styles.

DESIGNER: Isari Flower Studio
RECIPE: *Clematis* spp., *Dahlia* spp., *Paeonia* spp., *Pelargonium* spp., *Pieris japonica, Polystichum munitum, Rosa* spp.
"This was a bride's bouquet for a classic wedding. The bride wanted something modest to carry during her wedding ceremony."
PHOTOGRAPHER: The Grovers

DESIGN TIP

Though this is a versatile form, the round shape is a dominant display and creates a statement. Therefore, be attuned to the display setting to ensure the recipient or client would like such a powerful arrangement.

▶ *CIRCULAR MASS*
{Sub-Style}

Circular mass designs are round arrangements that use positive space as a dramatic element. The botanical materials are densely grouped within the round form to enhance the shape of the composition.

EURO ROUND
Designer/Photographer: Floral Art LA
Recipe: *Rosa* spp.
"This lush combination of red *Rosa* varieties features some blooms with reflexed petals. When *Rosa* petals are reflexed properly, it does not impact the longevity of the flower."

Euro Round designs are arranged with tightly compacted materials that are either highly organized to create a pattern (referred to as modern) or randomly placed (referred to as organic) within the form.

In weddings throughout European and American history, the circular mass style is the classic form of bridal bouquet. Sometimes referred to as a tussie-mussie or nosegay, this hand-held design became an integral component of floral design in the 1800s.

A transformation of the circular mass style can be shown in the oval form. An oval shape is an adaptation from the classic round sphere, where two sides of the circle are elongated.

HOLLOW ROUND

BIEDERMEIER

DESIGNER: Françoise Weeks
RECIPE: *Cosmos* spp., *Alchemilla mollis*, *Nigella* spp., *Celosia cristata*, *Hydrangea* spp., *Ageratum* spp., *Moluccella laevis*, *Adiantum capillus-veneris*, *Eucalyptus* spp. (pods), *Passiflora incarnata*, *Mentha* spp., *Anethum graveolens*, *Sambucus* spp., *Rubus fruticosus*, *Diospyros* spp.
PHOTOGRAPHER: Joni Shimabukuro

DESIGNER: The Flori.Culture
RECIPE: *Dianthus caryophyllus*, mollusks, rose quartz
"This is not your classic Biedermeier design. The use of shells and stones to create the rings as well as the pavé technique is a contemporary application of this traditional aesthetic."
PHOTOGRAPHER: Macey Sierka

▶ *HOLLOW ROUND*
{Sub-Style}

A hollow round is simply a circular form with negative space in the center of the design. Usually, the botanicals are placed together on the outer "rim" of the shape to create a halo effect. Application of this design is showcased in a traditional wreath design or flower crown.

The popular flower crowns of today are steeped in tradition and meaning. Review Roman and Grecian influence in floral design in the "Historic Periods of Floral Design" section *(Pages 88-95)*.

▶ *BIEDERMEIER*
{Sub-Style}

Biedermeier is a design created with concentric rings of materials to create a pattern. Each ring typically consists of only one type, variety or color of material. Making each ring different ensures that each circle stands out on its own. Materials used to create each ring can be botanicals or accent pieces such as shells or beads. Usually the design forms a dome or conical shape from a side view, but it can also be created using the pavé technique.

The Biedermeier composition originated in Germany and Austria between 1815 and 1848. The design was first displayed in furniture and paintings.

BIEDERMEIER MANDALA

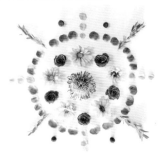

(Circular Form cont'd.)

The circular form is also showcased in the mandala trend. Mandalas are a spiritual symbol of the universe in Hinduism and Buddhism. They act as a chart to represent the cosmos, and, in Sanskrit translation, "mandala" means circle. Looking at the precise placement of botanicals in the mandala, it is easy to visualize the relationship and influence the mandala made on the Biedermeier style.

DESIGNER/PHOTOGRAPHER: Isari Flower Studio
RECIPE: *Chrysanthemum* spp., *Rosa* spp., *Leucospermum* spp., *Eucalyptus* spp.
"A mandala is an offering in the Buddhist and Hindu religions. It represents the universe and is used to focus attention and establish a sacred place. We often create them using floral scraps at the beginning of the week to set intention."`

TRIANGULAR FORM
[Style]

Triangular forms are among the most traditional of the geometric floral arrangement styles. To create this form, botanical materials are placed within a defined triangle framework applying either symmetrical or asymmetrical balance. Usually, the three points of the triangle are placed first, and then the additional botanicals are strategically placed to radiate from the focal point to the three outer points. Today, triangular floral arrangements are used quite often in event design, from centerpieces to altar décor. The triangle form is an adaptable shape.

DESIGNER: The Flori.Culture
RECIPE: *Dahlia spp.*
"The large *Dahlia* spp. blooms form the three points of the triangle with negative space in the center and between the three points. This simple yet elegant design is popular for the many corporate functions we design for."
PHOTOGRAPHER: Macey Sierka

(opposite page)
DESIGNER: The Flori.Culture
RECIPE: *Rosa* spp., *Eustoma* spp., *Craspedia globosa, Aspidistra elatior, Eucalyptus* spp., *Leucadendron* spp., *Monstera deliciosa, Rhapidophyllum hystrix, Xerophyllum tenax*
"The three points that make up the triangle in the arrangement are *Xerophyllum tenax* (far point on the left), *Eustoma* spp. on the top right, and *Monstera deliciosa* on the bottom right center. One may not automatically see the triangle at first glance, but after identification of these points, one can notice the arrangement's true form."
PHOTOGRAPHER: Macey Sierka

▶ *SYMMETRICAL TRIANGLE*
{Sub-Style}

The symmetrical triangle form is an exceptionally formal style. Symmetrically balanced triangles are either equilateral or isosceles. Equilateral triangles have three equal sides and are designed to be as tall as they are wide. Isosceles triangles have only two equal sides. These arrangements are either taller than they are wide (vertical triangles) or wider than they are tall (horizontal triangles).

❯ *T-shape Design*

The T-shape design is essentially an upside-down isosceles triangle. Two of the triangle points (the shorter line) are on the horizontal plane, and the third point of the triangle is below, pointing to the ground. Additionally, heavy use of negative space is highlighted between each of the three points in the triangle. Where the three points converge in the center of the arrangement is considered the focal point.

T-shape design

DESIGN TIP

In the most traditional triangular designs, smaller and lighter-colored flowers are used at the outer extremities, with larger and darker or brighter flowers used near the center of the triangle.

▶ ASYMMETRICAL TRIANGLE
{Sub-Style}

Asymmetrical triangles are scalene triangles, meaning they have three unequal sides. These scalene triangle designs have a vertical axis positioned off center, with materials placed unequally on each side. When divided vertically in half, one side may be visually heavier than the other. In comparison to symmetrical triangles, asymmetrical triangles are considered informal and appear less contrived.

Floral arrangements in these forms may be designed as obtuse, acute or right-angle triangles. Both obtuse and right-angle designs create a letter L shape *(see below)* while an acute scalene triangle resembles an unequal letter A.

❯ *L-shape Design*

A scalene triangle with a right (90-degree) angle is a formal letter L-shape design, and an obtuse angle is an informal, almost lazy L shape. L-shaped designs are characterized by the placement of materials in only two lines – vertical and horizontal – with the focal point where the two lines converge. Most important, this design is defined by the use of negative space between the vertical point and one of the horizontal points to ensure the shape of the letter L. The viewer of the arrangement must imaginatively create a dotted line between these vertical and horizontal points to create the shape of a triangle.

(opposite page)
DESIGNER: The Flori.Culture
RECIPE: *Acacia* spp., *Bougainvillea glabra*, *Cymbidium* spp., *Gossypium herbaceum*, *Nelumbo nucifera*, *Salix matsudana*, *Tillandsia xerographica*
"In this design, a shallow vessel on top of the wood pillar provides the mechanics to develop the long horizontal line and one vertical line of *Salix matsudana*. After the T shape was created, botanicals were placed on top of this frame but never in between the lines, to keep the T shape and enforce negative space."
PHOTOGRAPHER: Macey Sierka

DESIGNER/PHOTOGRAPHER: Lori McNorton
RECIPE: *Boronia* spp., *Dianthus caryophyllus*, *Jasminum* spp., *Matthiola incana*, *Moluccella laevis*, *Polystichum munitum*, *Rosa* spp.
"A colorful combination of linear and mass botanicals and foliage helps to create a beautiful fan-shaped arrangement."

FAN FORM
[Style]

The fan form may be thought of as a combination between a symmetrical triangle form and a circular form style. Fan designs are constructed using similar stem placements as a symmetrical triangle design, but the vertical component of the design is a radiating semicircle of lines that converge to create the focal point. Traditionally, fan forms are wider than they are tall, and the design on each side of the center axis should mirror itself, with identical materials and placements.

DESIGN TIP

Just as in a triangular design, the smaller and lighter-colored flowers are used traditionally at the outer extremities, with larger and darker or brighter flowers used nearer the center.

DESIGNER: Laura Dowling
RECIPE: *Dahlia* spp., *Fuchsia magellanica, Hedera helix, Hydrangea* spp., *Rosa* spp., *Tulipa* spp.
"In the summer style: a classic oval bouquet of bountiful seasonal flowers in an integrated organic vase."
PHOTOGRAPHER: Kevin Allen

▸ *POINTED OVAL*
  {Sub-Style}

Pointed-oval designs feature a fan shape but are heavily rounded and have one strong point of convergence. This sub-style is more elongated than regular ovals and resembles a symmetrical teardrop shape. The shape can be flipped in multiple directions, with the point of convergence facing vertically or horizontally.

DESIGNER: AZ Petal Pusher
RECIPE: *Delphinium elatum, Hydrangea macrophylla, Phalaenopsis amabilis, Tulipa* spp.
"The hybrid *Delphinium* are placed to create a strong back line, and on the lower level, a base is created with an array of white flowers including massed *Tulipa, Hydrangea* and *Phalaenopsis* to form a second parallel cluster."
PHOTOGRAPHER: Elyse Hall Photography

LINE FORM
[Style]

Line-form styles are a blend of minimalist Japanese ikebana and traditional massed arrangements of European floral influence. These blended arrangements highlight the element of line prominently. The lines appear in arrangements to be either straight (static line) or curved (dynamic line). Static lines are either vertical or horizontal, and dynamic lines create a diagonal, crescent, U shape or S shape. These styles lean to the more contemporary aesthetic, many of them are massed with a large quantity of florals highlighting positive space. Line styles are adaptable to many settings but are rigid in construction concepts.

▶ *VERTICAL*
{Static Line, Sub-Style}

Vertical botanical arrangements are designed in one line to move up and down. The standard rules of height proportions are extended beyond 1.5 times the height of the container for these designs, and many times in this style, a vessel is not used. These bold designs evoke a feeling of formality, dignity, power and strength.

DESIGNER: The Flori.Culture
RECIPE: *Caladium* spp., *Cymbidium* spp., *Craspedia globosa*, *Echeveria* spp., *Leucospermum* spp., *Phormium tenax*

"At The FloriCulture, we call these vertical line designs our hedge series arrangements. Their look is ultra contemporary but a statement design for modern weddings or corporate events. To create this vertical line, we insert stems of *Phormium tenax* into OASIS® Floral Foam Maxlife adjacent to one another and then cut the tops to create a straight horizontal line. Finally, we fill the base with other botanicals."
PHOTOGRAPHER: Macey Sierka

▶ *HORIZONTAL*
{Static Line, Sub-Style}

The horizontal-line style features botanicals that are parallel with the surfaces on which they are placed. The height of horizontal arrangements are low, and sometimes the sides of the arrangements may have a slight angle downward or upward, but this curve is not drastic enough to label the design U or crescent shaped. Just as in vertical designs, the standard rules of proportions are extended beyond 1.5 times the width of the container, and many times in this style, a vessel is not used. Horizontal designs are perceived to be stable, restful and tranquil.

DESIGNER: The Flori.Culture
RECIPE: *Anemone coronaria*, *Echeveria* spp., *Laurus nobilis*, *Ranunculus asiaticus*, *Rosa* spp., *Tulipa* spp.
PHOTOGRAPHER: Charity Maurer

"This trough arrangement ran the length of a wedding head table and was overflowing with *Tulipa* spp. and an assortment of garden blossoms. The glass vase trough is shaped in a horizontal line and depicts this form of line style superbly."

DESIGN TIP

A bird's-eye view of this arrangement assists in the symmetrical placement of botanicals. When designing, be sure not to taper the ends of the line too severely.

▶ *PARALLEL*
{Static Line, Sub-Style}

Parallel systems are simplistic designs that feature groups or clusters of linear botanicals with clean, strong vertical or horizontal lines. All of the stems in this style follow the same direction and are equidistant to one another. However, the heights of each group of materials may be varied though they are running parallel to other clusters of species. In traditional parallel-system designs, each group consists of only one type of botanical species, and all materials should be within the edges of the container.

DESIGNER: The Flori.Culture
RECIPE: *Rosa* spp.
"The placement of tall linear bud vases in a zigzag formation, with *Rosa* spp. stems cut at the same height, creates a parallel system of blooms lifted to the same dimensional plane."
PHOTOGRAPHER: Macey Sierka

▶ NEW CONVENTION
{Static Line, Sub-Style}

The new-convention sub-style is identified by the use of parallel systems with both vertical and horizontal stem placements in the arrangement. Each parallel group of materials is placed either vertically or horizontally, with negative space between them. The horizontally placed botanical groups are shorter and are situated at 90-degree angles to the vertical materials, and they extend beyond the edge of the container.

DESIGNER/PHOTOGRAPHER: John Regan, Ph.D.
RECIPE: *Zantedeschia aethiopica, Liriope muscari*
"The minimal amount of material in this composition allows the viewer to appreciate the contrast between the static structure versus the dynamic lines. The black vintage-inspired flower frog, typically concealed within a deeper vase, is shown in full display in a lox black porcelain dish. Its white interior is repeated in the twisting *Zantedeschia* spp. and the *Liriope* spp. stems looped and racing through the form to accentuate the playfulness."

▶ *DIAGONAL*
{Dynamic Line, Sub-Style}

Diagonal-line floral arrangements are generally situated on a 45-degree angle to a horizontal plane. These tilted lines prompt eye movement, creating an energetic and powerful feeling, but they also may conjure tension or instability.

DESIGNER/PHOTOGRAPHER: John Regan, Ph.D.
RECIPE: *Citrus* x *clementina*, *Hydrangea* spp., *Leucospermum cordifolium*, *Passiflora incarnata*, *Phalaenopsis amabilis*
"This diagonal design features grouped flowers with attention to boldly contrasting colors and textures."

▶ *WATERFALL OR CASCADE*
{Dynamic Line, Sub-Style}

Waterfall, or cascade, designs are a fashionably organic aesthetic. They are created with many layers of botanical materials, often foliage, placed upon each other in a steep downward flow in which the line is usually slightly curved. This style can be created in both container arrangements and bouquets to carry. This style became popular in Europe in the 1800s and has sustained popularity through today.

DESIGNER: The Flori.Culture
RECIPE: *Rosa* spp., *Passiflora incarnata*, *Ilex* spp., *Citrus* × *paradisi*
PHOTOGRAPHER: Macey Sierka

"*Passiflora incarnata* is a very simple botanical to drape in the cascade form to create a waterfall design. It blends well with many other botanical species and creates a tropical yet garden aesthetic. At The Flori.Culture, we usually design this style for areas that need high impact, such as ceremony, stage, or bar décor."

DESIGN TIP

To create the long, flowing form of a waterfall or cascade arrangement, use botanicals that are pendulous and have a natural curve or long pliable stems; line-form botanicals and vining foliage are best.

U-SHAPE

DESIGNER/PHOTOGRAPHER: John Regan, Ph.D.
RECIPE: *Anigozanthos* spp., *Aronia melanocarpa, Celosia* spp., *Dahlia* spp., *Foeniculum vulgare, Sedum/Hylotelephium telephium, Malus* spp., *Schinus molle, Smilax* spp.
"Texture is the driving energy in this analogous design. The upward crescent form allows the gold-toned compote to add a metallic aspect that helps to catch light."

▸ *CRESCENT OR C- OR U-SHAPE DESIGN*
{Dynamic Line, Sub-Style}

As either of these names suggests, crescent or U-shape designs mimic the curve of the moon (first or last quarter phase) or the letters C or U. Their shape forms a circle or an oval, with some mass in the center and tapering to points at both ends. This sub-style is created through the use of negative space and looks as though a bite or a scoop has been taken out of a round. These designs can be created vertically, to look like the shape of the letter C (or a backward C) or a crescent moon, or horizontally, to look like the letter U. Furthermore, these designs may be either symmetrically or asymmetrically balanced, and their lines may be ascending (upward-curving) or descending (downward-curving.) The ascending line is traditional for container arrangements, and descending is traditional for hand-held bouquets. The asymmetrical U-shape (or horizontal letter C or crescent) is a popular style for event centerpieces.

DESIGN TIP
For a true crescent shape, asymmetrical balance is promoted with the tip of the longer line extending to either directly above or below the focal point.

HOGARTH / S-SHAPE

DESIGNER: Nancy Zimmerman
RECIPE: *Antirrhinum majus, Asparagus
setaceus, Eucalyptus polyanthemos,
Eustoma grandiflorum, Hydrangea
macrophylla, Ruscus aculeatus,
Ranunculus asiaticus., Rosa* spp.,
Scabiosa spp., *Veronica spicata*
"This is my first Hogarth curve
arrangement and I designed it in my floral
intensive with Holly Heider Chapel at
Hope Flower Farm."
PHOTOGRAPHER: Rebekah J. Murray

▶ *HOGARTH OR S-SHAPE DESIGN*
{Dynamic Line, Sub-Style}

The Hogarth curve is a design in the shape of the letter S. This shape is best visualized as two ascending and descending semicircles, one placed atop the other, curving in opposite directions. A dominant focal point is created from these merging semicircles.
In a Hogarth curve's truest form, the tip of the ascending line is directly above the focal point, and the tip of the descending line is directly below the focal point. Though this style is lovely and has a historic flare, it is relatively uncommon today.

The Hogarth curve is named for the English painter, William Hogarth, who described it in his text *The Analysis of Beauty*, published in 1753. In this book, Mr. Hogarth theorized that the serpentine line was the "basis for all successful artistic design" and that all artistic beauty developed from this line.

DESIGN TIP
Restraint in using a large quantity of botanicals is key.
Organization and control are essential in formal-linear designs.

DESIGNER: The Flori.Culture
RECIPE: *Paeonia* spp., *Echinacea* spp.,
*Asparagus setaceus, Cotinus coggygria,
Salix matsudana, Trachelospermum
jasminoides*
"Each flower and foliage position is key to creating this very specific design style. When designing this type of arrangement, we apply negative space and proportional stem lengths to the vessel to ensure that strategic placement is adhered to."
PHOTOGRAPHER: Macey Sierka

▶ *FORMAL-LINEAR*
{Dynamic Line, Sub-Style}

The formal-linear sub-style is defined by distinct curved or straight vertical, horizontal and diagonal lines placed in a precise manner. With heavy use of negative space between botanical materials, these lines converge at the focal point of the arrangement. Materials are typically arranged asymmetrically in groups, and minimal amounts of each material are used so that the form, color, texture, pattern and beauty of each material, as well as the lines each creates, are accentuated. These clean, distinct lines create a feeling of movement, and the emphasis is on showcasing distinctive materials and shapes.

Formal-linear designs were popular in the 1980s and 1990s and are of German origin as a hybrid of historic Japanese and European design styles.

INNOVATIVE STYLES
Interpretive/Free-form, Abstract

Innovative floral arrangements are styles that reflect a new method of construction or display. They do not have a defined form to follow, and they require a great deal of skillful artistry and imagination. Innovative designs are achieved through a well-developed design process and the practice of creativity.

(above)
DESIGNER: Merveille Floral & Design
RECIPE: *Delphinium* spp., *Dendrobium* spp., *Hydrangea macrophylla, Phalaenopsis amabilis, Populus tremuloides, Rosa* spp., *Symphoricarpos albus*
"For this opulent wedding bar design, we created a distinctive and innovative 'floral tree' in crisp white, set on a genuine *Populus* tree trunk."
PHOTOGRAPHER: John Cane Studio

(left)
DESIGNER: Merveille Floral & Design
RECIPE: *Dianthus caryophyllus*
"We designed this unique mandap for a wedding ceremony in which the ring structure is suspended and draped with necklaces of carnations."

▸ *INTERPRETIVE/FREE-FORM*
[Style]

Interpretive, free-form floral designs are unconventional and unique works based on imagination. The designs can reflect realistic or nonrealistic aesthetics, and there is no set form. However, correct application of the elements and principles still must be displayed.

▸ *ABSTRACT*
[Style]

Abstract means nonrealistic or theoretical. The abstract botanical arrangement style showcases out-of-the-box ideas and requires a great deal of creativity and imagination. Essentially, there are no rules to follow. However, note that it takes great skill and practice to create a well-developed abstract work.

(opposite page)
DESIGNER: Edith Guzmán Díaz, EMC
RECIPE: *Agave sisalana, Cocos nucifera, Eucalyptus globulus, Viola x wittrockiana*
"'Love' is a floral composition that recalls the love between two people. The kiss is the connection that this feeling cause."
PHOTOGRAPHER: Manuel Barragán

HISTORICAL PERIODS
OF FLORAL DESIGN

Egyptian, Grecian, Roman, Byzantine, Japanese, Renaissance, Baroque and Dutch Flemish, Colonial, Georgian, Victorian and Romantic, Rococo, Art Nouveau, Art Deco

The historical periods of floral design are an important study because many of the techniques and styles florists apply today are inherited from designers past. Essentially, a review of the history of floral design is the practice of floral art appreciation and is a source of inspiration for today's popular styles.

DESIGNER/PHOTOGRAPHER: John Regan, Ph.D.
RECIPE: *Caltha palustris, Campanula* 'Cherry Bells', *Carduus acanthoides, Hydrangea* spp., *Malus* foliage, *Nelumbo nucifera, Phalaenopsis* spp., *Sandersonia* spp.
"Even though I frequently design/build exceedingly large and lush designs on any given day, designs such as this are a result of my appreciation for material with slender (almost ephemeral) stems. Hold a stem of *Sandersonia* or *Caltha* in your hand and it's almost weightless. Contrast that with the bigger blooms of *Hydrangea, Nelumbo* and *Carduus* for more visual weight at the base of the design, and the slender stems extending out remind me of fireworks."

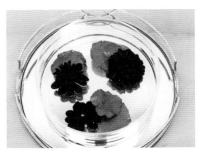

DESIGNER: The Flori.Culture
RECIPE: *Dahlia* spp., *Galax urceolata*
PHOTOGRAPHER: Macey Sierka

▶ *EGYPTIAN*

2800 B.C. - 28 B.C.

Artifacts indicate that the ancient Egyptian civilization cut botanicals to use for aesthetic purposes. Flowers and foliage were used in vessels as ornamental home décor as well as for personal adornment. Botanicals were exhibited for spiritual and religious ceremonies.

"The *Dahlia* spp. is representative of the water-lily flower (*Nymphaea* spp.), and the *Galax urceolata* represents the lily pads in this arrangement. This type of floating arrangement is an example of what was created by Egyptians in bowls and basins for display during ceremonies."

▶ *GRECIAN*

600 B.C. - 146 B.C.

This civilization was the first to recognize the florist profession. The Greeks wore garlands and wreaths as a form of symbolism in their culture. The cornucopia was introduced in this period as well as the custom of strewing petals upon the ground for ceremonial purposes.

DESIGNER: Susan McLeary
RECIPE: *Lophomyrtus* leaves
"This simple crown was made by gluing individual *Lophomyrtus* leaves onto bullion wire. Simple and delicate but impactful and reminiscent of a Grecian adornment."
PHOTOGRAPHER: Erin Schmidt Photography

DESIGNER: The Flori.Culture
RECIPE: *Laurus nobilis, Olea europaea*
PHOTOGRAPHER: Macey Sierka

▶ *ROMAN*

28 B.C. - A.D. 325

The Romans adopted the custom of wearing garlands and wreaths from the Greeks. Fragrance and color were the two most popular elements of the time. Rose petals, in particular, were abundantly strewn throughout elaborate banquets and festivals.

"People in both the Greek and Roman cultures wore head wreaths in their daily lives. Many were given as a symbolic honor or as an award for an accomplished work."

▶ *BYZANTINE*
A.D. 330 - A.D. 527

Mosaics depict the floral arrangement styles of the time. Conical, triangular arrangements were designed using symmetrical balance. Thinner, spiraling garlands were created with both flowers and foliage.

DESIGNER: Susan McLeary
RECIPE: *Athyrium niponicum, Cornus florida, Convallaria majalis, Lamprocapnos spectabilis, Polygonatum* spp., *Ranunculus asiaticus, Spiraea* spp.
PHOTOGRAPHER: Jennifer Ilene Photography

▶ *JAPANESE*
A.D. 586 - Current

Ikebana is the practice of floral art in Japan, but the form had its start in China. Japanese designs are a form of symbolism and are spiritual, suggestive and meaningful. Designs are minimalistic in nature and are formed using strict rules of ornamentation.

DESIGNER: Hitomi Gilliam, AIFD, EMC
RECIPE: *Amaranthus caudatus, Dahlia pinnata* 'Burma Gem', *Daucus carota* 'Chocolate Lace', *Dianthus caryophyllus* 'Terracotta Caramel', *Jasminum officinale, Nandina domestica, Rosa* spp. 'Cappuccino', *Rosa* spp. 'Wanted', *Ranunculus* spp., *Scabiosa atropurpurea* 'Double Red'
"Japanese fan with *Bambusa* spines decorated with rich floral tapestry in an obi-like band."
PHOTOGRAPHER: Colin Gilliam

▶ *RENAISSANCE (EUROPEAN)*
A.D. 1400 - A.D. 1600

The resurgence of the arts after the Middle Ages greatly impacted the art of floral design. Europeans inherited styles and techniques from the Greek and Roman florists. Paintings of florals from this time are heavily concentrated on religious symbolism. Designs were constructed in a compact mass fashion, in a conical or pointed-oval shape.

DESIGNER/PHOTOGRAPHER: John Regan, Ph.D.
RECIPE: *Ageratum houstonianum, Hippeastrum* spp. 'Exotic Nymph', *Hydrangea* spp., *Ligustrum vulgare, Phalaenopsis amabilis, Syringa vulgaris*
"Rolled ball of chicken wire secured within the metal compote supports these heavy (and in the case of the *Hippeastrum*, hollow) stems. The wire framework allows the stems to have direct access to a large volume of water, adding to the vase life of the design. Several of the heavy-headed flowers at the perimeter of the design are weighted at the bottom of their stems to prevent them from pulling out of the design. The design is built by inserting the flowers with the widest or heaviest stems first. So here the *Hippeastrum* were added first, then the *Hydrangea, Syringa, Viburnum*, etc. The *Phalaenopsis* are the final addition. To allow all the varied flowers have the contributing impact, stems are grouped and color is inspired by Imari porcelain."

▶ *BAROQUE (ITALIAN) AND FLEMISH (DUTCH)*
A.D. 1550 - A.D. 1700

The economic climate of this period allowed for continued growth in floral design. The art of floral design became more appreciated and accessible. Baroque and Flemish arrangement styles were ornate, elaborate and detailed. Styles were overflowing with many botanical types showcased in one design. The arrangement styles of the time are captured in Dutch-Flemish paintings though many of these painters did not arrange flowers but simply imagined the designs they painted.

DESIGNER: The Flori.Culture
RECIPE: *Chamelaucium uncinatum, Cotinus coggygria, Delphinium* spp., *Eucalyptus* spp.
"The floral arrangements designed in this period were overflowing with a variety of garden blooms, and an emphasis on curved lines within the arrangements was popular. This design highlights the style with an asymmetry in balance and line, and it showcases the ornate detailing in the silver pedestal container, which was also favored."
PHOTOGRAPHER: Macey Sierka

▶ *COLONIAL (AMERICAN)*
A.D. 1620 - A.D. 1780

This style originated in Williamsburg, the capital of the Virginia colonies. Form styles of round and fan shapes were popular. These arrangements had a formal yet wildflower-like aesthetic.

DESIGNER: The Flori.Culture
RECIPE: *Achillea millefolium, Anemone coronaria, Echinacea* spp., *Lysimachia nemorum, Scabiosa* spp., *Serruria florida*
"In the Colonial style, this arrangement showcases dried and fresh botanicals. The fan-shaped milk-glass vessel was specifically designed for the display of flowers and foliage."
PHOTOGRAPHER: Macey Sierka

▶ *GEORGIAN (ENGLISH)*
A.D. 1714 - A.D. 1760

Fragrant botanicals were very important during this period because it was believed that the pleasant aroma of flowers could clean the air (from disease and stench). Due to the importance of fragrance, nosegays or tussie-mussies (hand-held bouquets) became all the rage for women to carry. During this time, it is believed that use of traditional bud vases and formal dining centerpieces began.

(opposite page)
DESIGNER: Laura Dowling
RECIPE: *Buxus sempervirens, Dahlia* spp., *Delphinium* spp., *Hedera helix, Hydrangea* spp., *Rosa* spp., *Veronica arvensis*
"A classically elegant bouquet in the Georgian style makes a striking statement in the morning light."
PHOTOGRAPHER: Kevin Allen

DESIGNER: Laura Dowling
RECIPE: *Dahlia* spp., *Helianthus annuus, Rosa* spp., *Zinnia elegans, Hedera helix*
"Bouquets of *Helianthus annuus, Zinnia elegans, Dahlia* spp. and *Rosa* spp. in a moody palette are arranged in the Victorian style, with abundant masses of flowers and free-flowing lines."
PHOTOGRAPHER: Sunni Kim Cook

▶ *VICTORIAN (ENGLISH) AND ROMANTIC (AMERICAN)*
A.D. 1830 - A.D. 1890

This era in floral design history was one of the most impactful because this was the first time in Europe that established rules of floral arranging were noted in books and magazines. American floral arrangements copied the designs and practices prevalent in England. Plants were popular in everyday life, and young women learned to arrange flowers and grow botanicals as well as dry and paint flowers. The arrangement style of the time was overflowing with a compact assortment of blooms in round or oval forms. The nosegay/tussie-mussie trend was still popular, and the "Language of Flowers" evolved in this time. The "Language of Flowers" was developed from the custom of a young man giving a nosegay of flowers to a young women for her to carry, wherein each flower had a particular meaning associated with it. It was a tradition of courting or dating.

▶ ROCOCO (FRENCH)
A.D. 1715 - A.D. 1744

Floral arrangements reflecting Flemish styles were displayed for Louis XIV, King of France and Navarra from 1643 to 1715. The styles were ornate, to represent luxury and aristocracy. Forms of the arrangements at this time were fan or triangular in shape.

DESIGNER: John Regan, Ph.D.
RECIPE: *Dahlia* spp., *Nerine sarniensis, Gomphrena globosa, Lilium* spp., *Hydrangea macrophylla* 'White Magic', *Ornithogalum arabicum, Clematis* spp.
"The achromatic collection of blooms allow the mercury-glass compote to take center stage. Like most any monochromatic design, selection of stems is based on presenting contrasting forms and textures to provide interest. This design is made with the aid of a kenzan-style pin holder to secure a tightly packed mix. In contrast, the slender meandering stems of *Clematis* spp. vine provide implied movement. This type of design can be a profitable way to utilize shorter or broken stems."
PHOTOGRAPHER: Amy O'Brien

▶ ART NOUVEAU (AMERICAN & EUROPEAN)
A.D. 1880 - A.D. 1925

Creativity in floral design was embraced during this time. Abundantly filled, curved and asymmetrical designs depicting nature were popular.

DESIGNER: Susan McLeary
RECIPE: *Achillea millefolium, Amaranthus retroflexus, Astilbe* spp., *Banksia* spp., *Begonia* x *semperflorens-cultorum, Clematis* spp., *Continus coggygria, Heuchera* spp., *Hydrangea* spp., *Ribes* spp., *Rubus idaeus*
"Highly ornate and decorative, with swirling tendrils and gilded berries, this Art Nouveau-inspired headpiece is a celebration of the natural elements and curved lines that marked this period."
PHOTOGRAPHER: Amanda Dumouchelle Photography

▶ ART DECO (AMERICAN & FRENCH)
A.D. 1925 - A.D. 1930

This era began in Paris, France, at the 1925 World's Fair, the *"Exposition Internationale des Arts Décoratifs et Industriels Modernes."* Floral designs were influenced by a wide range of new concepts and scientific achievements. Modern styles with geometric forms were introduced.

DESIGNER: Isari Flower Studio
RECIPE: *Echeveria* spp., *Echinops sphaerocephalus, Jacobaea maritima, Salix matsudana, Zantedeschia aethiopica*
"This Art Deco bridal bouquet is a contemporary approach to the 1920s floral fashion. The *Zantedeschia aethiopica* and *Salix matsudana* evoke timeless elegance and are accentuated with architectural *Echinops sphaerocephalus* and *Echeveria* spp."
PHOTOGRAPHER: Paula Luna

The richness I achieve comes from nature, the source of my inspiration.

– Claude Monet

In my study of floral design as an art form, I have concluded that floral design stands for our appreciation of the most natural art form: nature itself. As botanical artists, our adoration for nature and its beauty is the reason we create art.

Flower arranging is truly the most organic of all artistic endeavors, with flowers as our medium for artistic expression. Yes, the elements and principles of design, as well as the techniques, are important to developing harmonious compositions. But really, floral design is about communicating joy through natural elements.

I hope this book inspires you to delve deeper into the practice of floral artistry. Keep being inspired, and go play with flowers.

Bloom on!

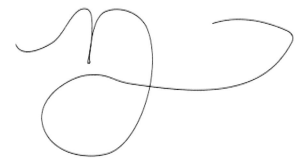

Morgan Anderson, Ph.D.
Botanical Artist and Educator
The Flori.Culture
Scottsdale, Arizona

WORKS CITED

Cameron, J. (2016). *The Artist's Way: A Spiritual Path to Higher Creativity*. New York, NY: TarcherPerigee.

Hunter, N.T. (2000). *The Art of Floral Design*. Albany, NY: Delmar.

Johnson, J.L., McKinley, W.J., & Benz, M. (2001). *Flowers: Creative Design*. College Station, TX: Texas A&M University Press, San Jacinto Publishing Company.

Vande Zande, R.V., Warnock, L., Nikoomanesh, B., & Dexter, K.V. (2014). *The Design Process in the Art Classroom: Building Problem Solving-Skills For Life and Careers*. Art Education, 67(6), 20-27.

PUBLISHER: Travis Rigby

AUTHORS: Morgan Anderson, Ph.D.; David Coake; Shelley Urban; Teresa Lanker

EDITORS: Morgan Anderson, Ph.D.; David Coake

CONTRIBUTING FLORAL DESIGNERS: AZ Petal Pusher; Edith Guzmán Díaz, EMC; Floral Art LA; Françoise Weeks; Hitomi Gilliam, AIFD, EMC; Isari Flower Studio; John Regan, Ph.D.; Laura Dowling; Lori McNorton; Merveille Floral & Design; Nancy Teasley/Oak & the Owl; Nancy Zimmerman; Natasha Lisitsa and Daniel Schultz; Pigsty Studio; Susan McLeary; The Flori.Culture

CONTRIBUTING PHOTOGRAPHERS: Amanda Dumouchelle Photography; Amber Snow; Amy O'Brien; Brealyn Nenes; Charity Maurer; Colin Gilliam; Elyse Hall Photography; Erin Beach; Erin Schmidt Photography; Floral Art LA; Hannah Costello Photography; Hope Sword; Isari Flower Studio; Jamie Bosworth; Jennifer Ilene Photography; John Cane Studio; John Regan, Ph.D.; Joni Shimabukuro; Kevin Allen; Lori McNorton; Macey Sierka; Manuel Barragán; Paula Luna; Rebekah J. Murray; Shane and Lauren Photography; Sunni Kim Cook; The Grovers

ART DIRECTOR: Kathleen Dillinger

GRAPHIC DESIGNER: Christina Ferris

Printed in China

ISBN-13: 978-0-9854743-8-6